The Adventures of Beckham Grey
THE
FARM CHALLENGE

ISBN: 979-8-9885419-1-2

Quail Acres Publishing
Imagination is Priceless!

www.elizabethalfheim.com

Printed and bound in the United States of America

A to Z Practice

Practice writing your letters by tracing the ones below. Can you sing the alphabet too?

Aa Bb Cc Dd Ee Ff

Gg Hh Ii Jj Kk Ll

Mm Nn Oo Pp Qq

Rr Ss Tt Uu Vv Ww

Xx Yy Zz

Good job! Now try it again.

Aa Bb Cc Dd Ee Ff

Gg Hh Ii Jj Kk Ll

Mm Nn Oo Pp Qq

Rr Ss Tt Uu Vv

Ww Xx Yy Zz

Add 'Em Up

Count each group of pictures, add 'em up, and write the correct answer in the box.

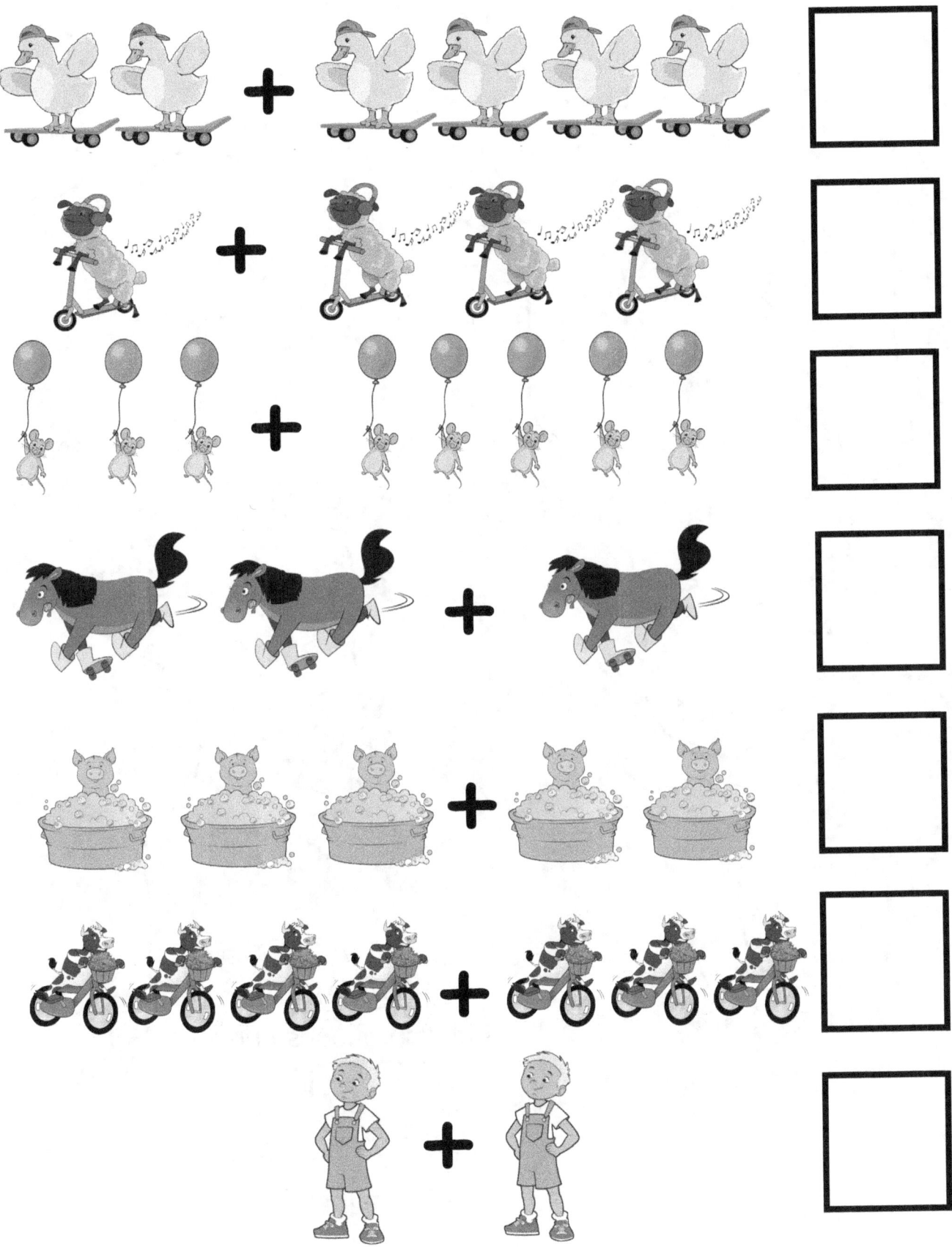

Color 7 Balloons

Then count how many balloons are NOT colored.
Write your answer in the box.

There are SEVEN
colored balloons and

[   ]

balloons that are
NOT colored.

Animal Tracks

Directions: Draw a picture of the animal tracks for each farm animal.

Cow

Pony

Goose

Chicken

Pig

Sheep

??
Draw what you think they look like.

1 to 10 Practice

Practice writing your numbers and words by tracing the ones below. Count the objects in each line.

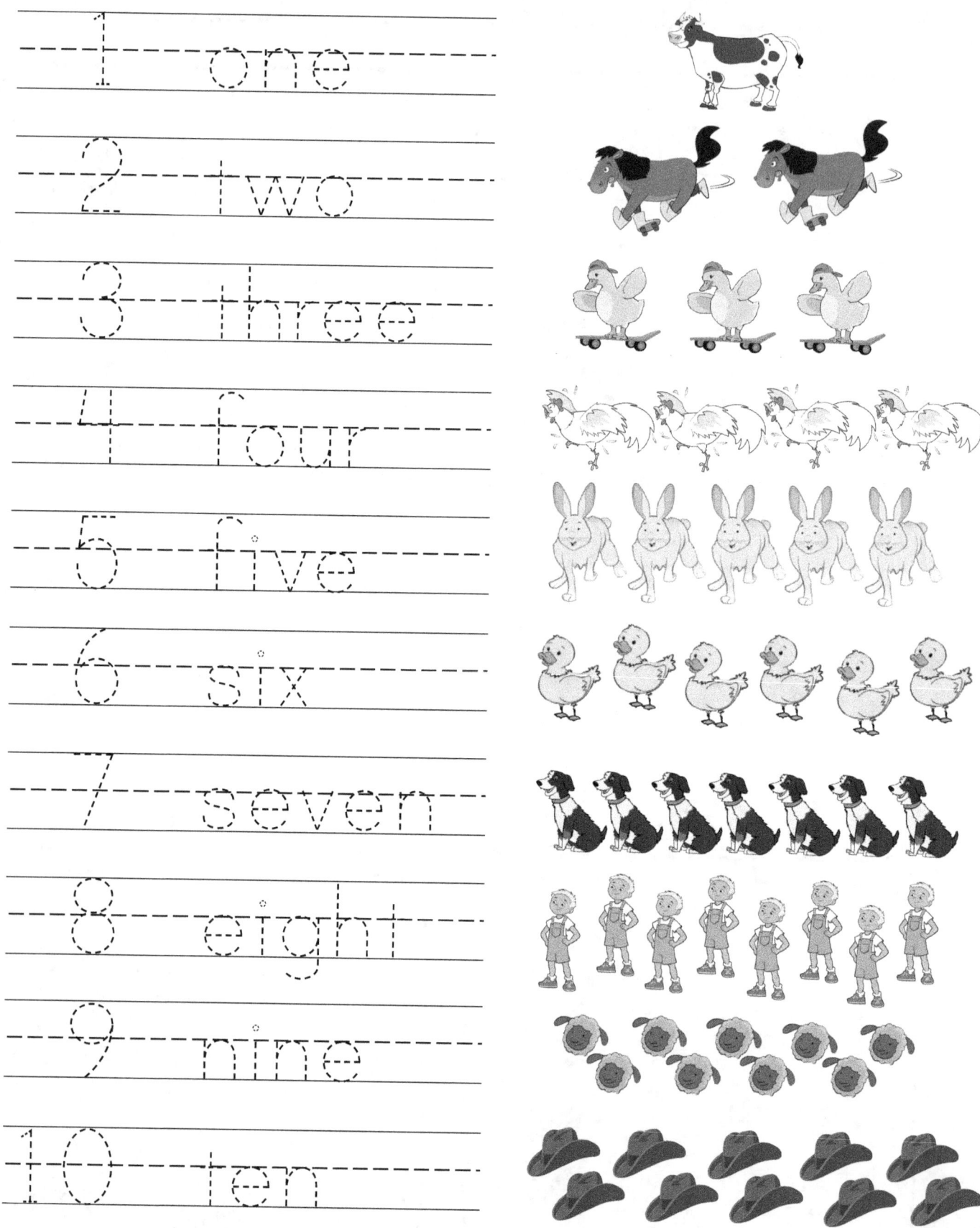

1 one

2 two

3 three

4 four

5 five

6 six

7 seven

8 eight

9 nine

10 ten

Adding 10

Connect the geese to the correct skateboard by adding ten.
Use the counting bar if you need help.

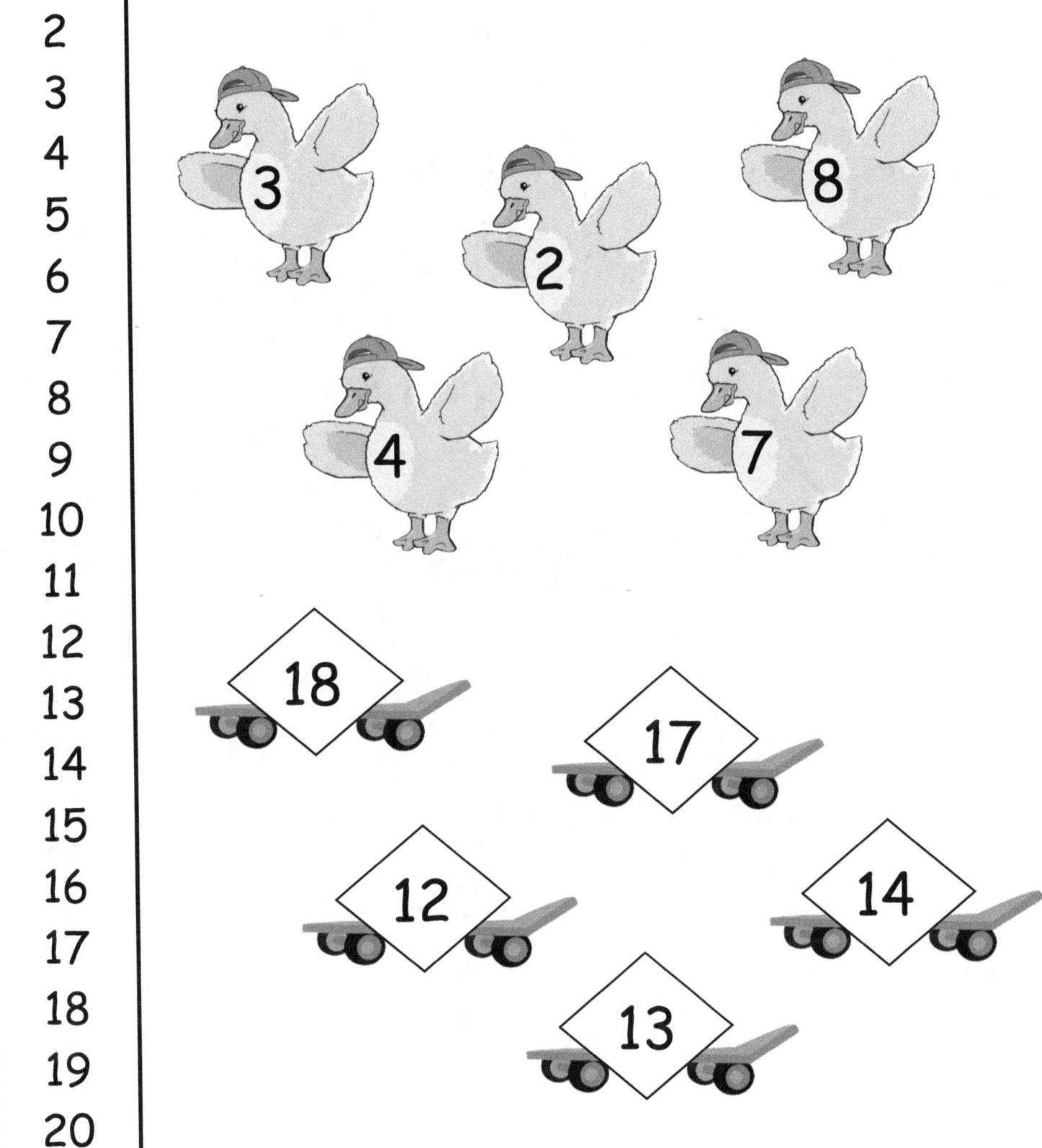

Balloon Math

7- RED   8 - BLUE   9 - GREEN   10 - YELLOW

Alphabet Pairs

Draw a line to the matching letters to give Rat back his balloon.

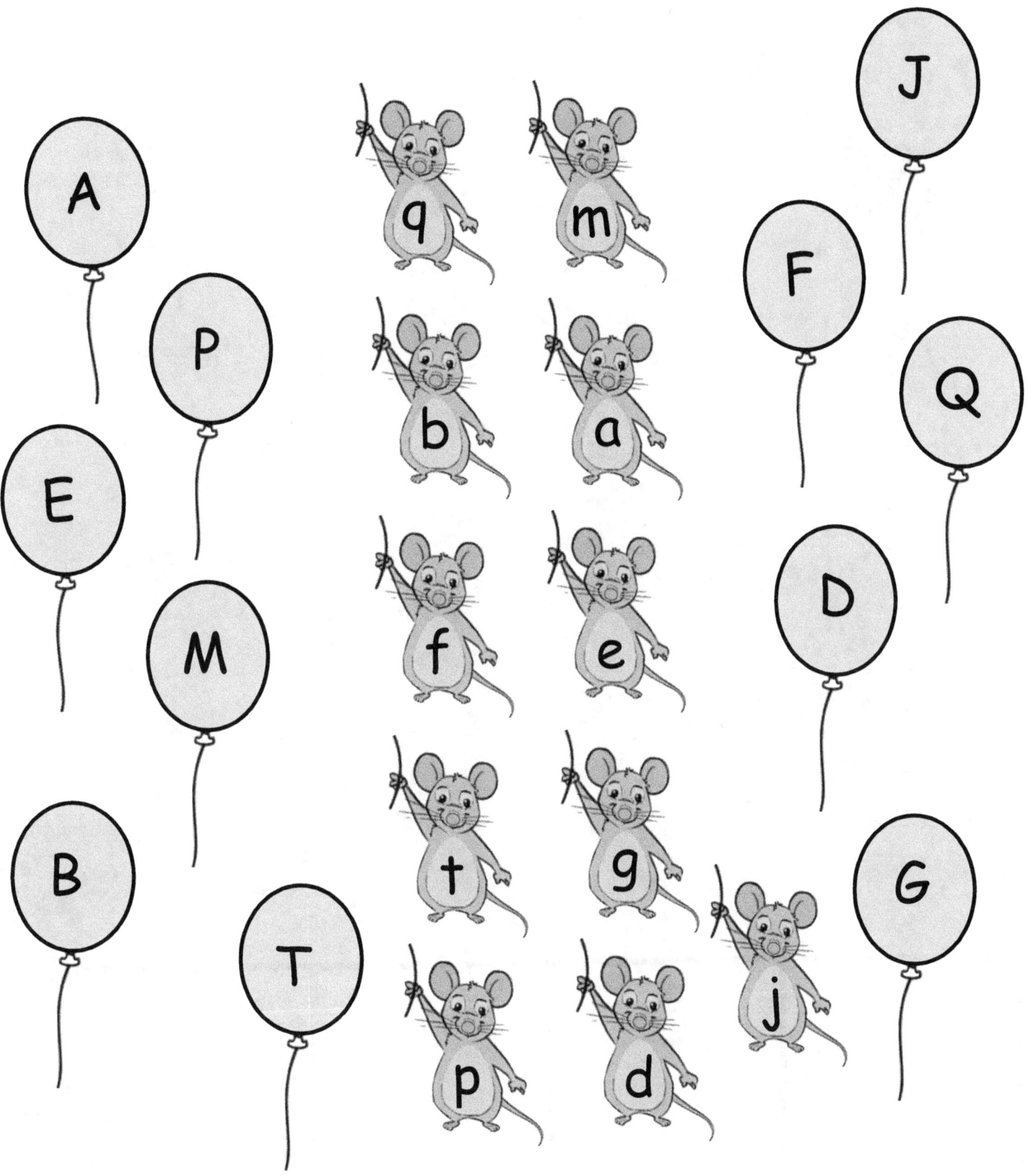

Beckham's Farm Challenge

How many animals are on Beckham's farm? Put a tally mark in the boxes below for each animal you count. Cross out the animal once it has been counted. The first one is done for you.

	I		

A Different Point of View

Artists create different points of view through their drawings. Look at the two drawings below. What catches your eye that's different between them? Describe as many differences as you can find.

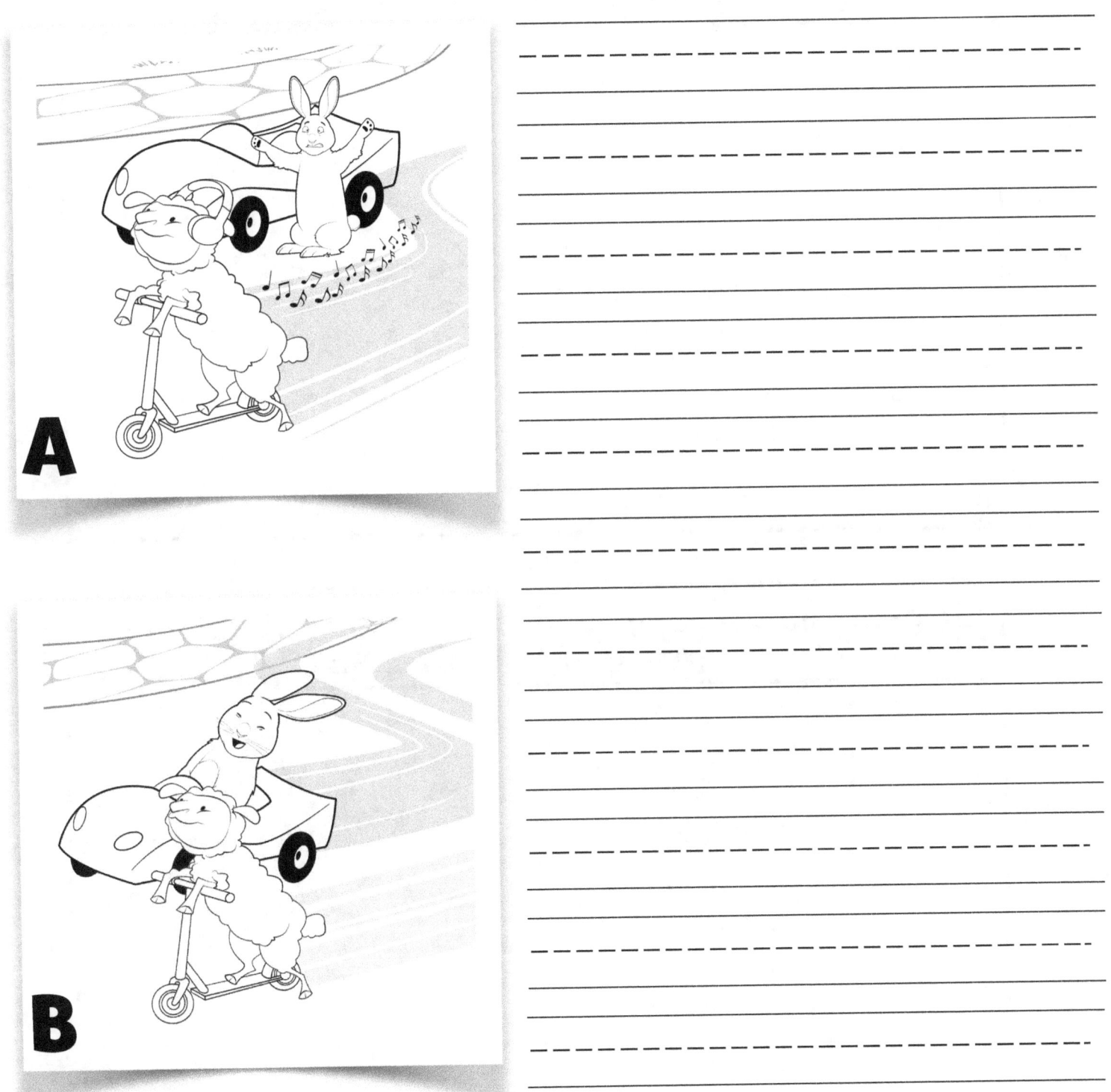

I found _____ differences.

A Picture is Worth A Thousand Words

For each word, read the description.
Then draw a picture that shows the word in action.

Pled: Appealed; petitioned; begged.
"I'd rather go swimming," the duckling pled.

Tug-of-war: A competition of strength using a rope.
Your challenge will be a farm tug-of-war.

BEFORE - Between - AFTER

Write the number that comes before, between, and after each number below.

BEFORE	Between	AFTER
___ 11	3 ___ 5	7 ___
___ 6	9 ___ 11	19 ___
___ 14	1 ___ 3	2 ___
___ 19	14 ___ 16	11 ___
___ 5	7 ___ 9	8 ___
___ 2	18 ___ 20	16 ___
___ 10	6 ___ 8	5 ___

Circle the beginning sound for each object.

D B P V

B G H T

L D V B

T J K L

L A V S

S C B Z

Beginning Sounds

Write the beginning sound for each picture. Then sound out the word.

_____ ig

_____ ub

_____ oose

_____ kates

_____ ow

_____ ike

Which Is Bigger?

Circle the biggest animals in each row.

1, 2, 3 Practice

Practice writing your numbers by tracing the ones below. Then try a couple on your own.

1   1   1

2   2   2

3   3   3

4   4   4

5   5   5

6   6   6

7   7   7

Good job!
Circle your best number in each row.

8   8   8

9   9   9

10   10   10

A-Mazing Flying Chicken

Then a high-pitched humming was heard overhead.
Chicken, dropped by a drone, was screaming off her head.
Help Chicken find her way safely to Beckham Grey.

Color Challenge!

Follow the instructions for coloring the picture.

Pink: pig, Gigi (face, arms, legs), Beckham (face arms, legs, neck), pony (inside ear, mouth), rabbit (inside ears, mouth), rat (tail, ears), dog (mouth), cow (inside ears, nose)

Brown: fence, walkway

Green: grass, shrubs

Light blue: sky, rat, Beckham's overalls

Gray: chicken (tail feathers, face), sheep, goose

Black: pony mane, pig hooves, sheep face, dog nose

Red: Gigi's shirt, chicken comb, dog collar

Orange: goose (beak, feet)

Draw patches on cow and dog. Color them **black**.

Color the picture using the color key below.

Color Key

1 = pink   2 = gray   3 = blue
4 = black   5 = red   6 = yellow
7 = light blue

Count How Many

Count how many items are in each box. Color in the correct number.
Is it 7,8, or 9?

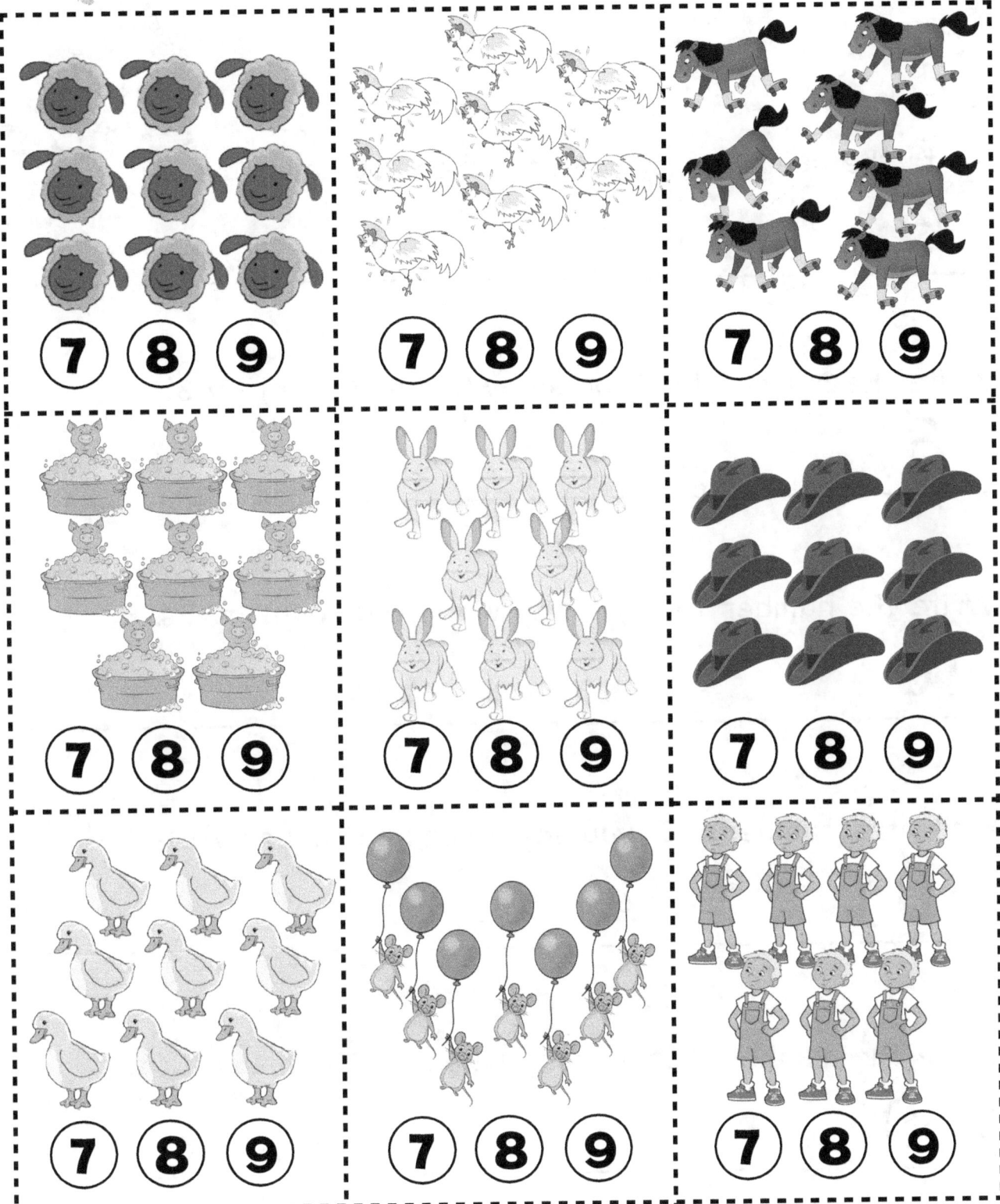

Counting by...

3's 2's 10's 5's 100's

Write the number that you say when you count by 2's.

<u>6</u> ___ ___ ___ ___ ___

Write the number that you say when you count by 3's.

<u>6</u> ___ ___ ___ ___ ___

Write the number that you say when you count by 5's.

<u>10</u> ___ ___ ___ ___ ___

Write the number that you say when you count by 10's.

<u>10</u> ___ ___ ___ ___ ___

Write the number that you say when you count by 100's.

<u>100</u> ___ ___ ___ ___ ___

Colorful Shapes

squares - **red** circles - **blue**
triangles - **yellow** rectangles - **green**

Consonant Blends

ch   gr   sc   sk

Using the letter combinations above, fill in the correct consonant blend on each line. Then draw a line from the word to the correct picture.

_____ icken

_____ ooter

_____ ates

_____ ateboard

Beckham _____ ey

Draw a line to connect the matching ponies.

Ducks in a Pool

Count the ducks in the pool with goggles. Count how many ducks got out of the pool and took off their goggles. Subtract to tell how many are still in the pool.

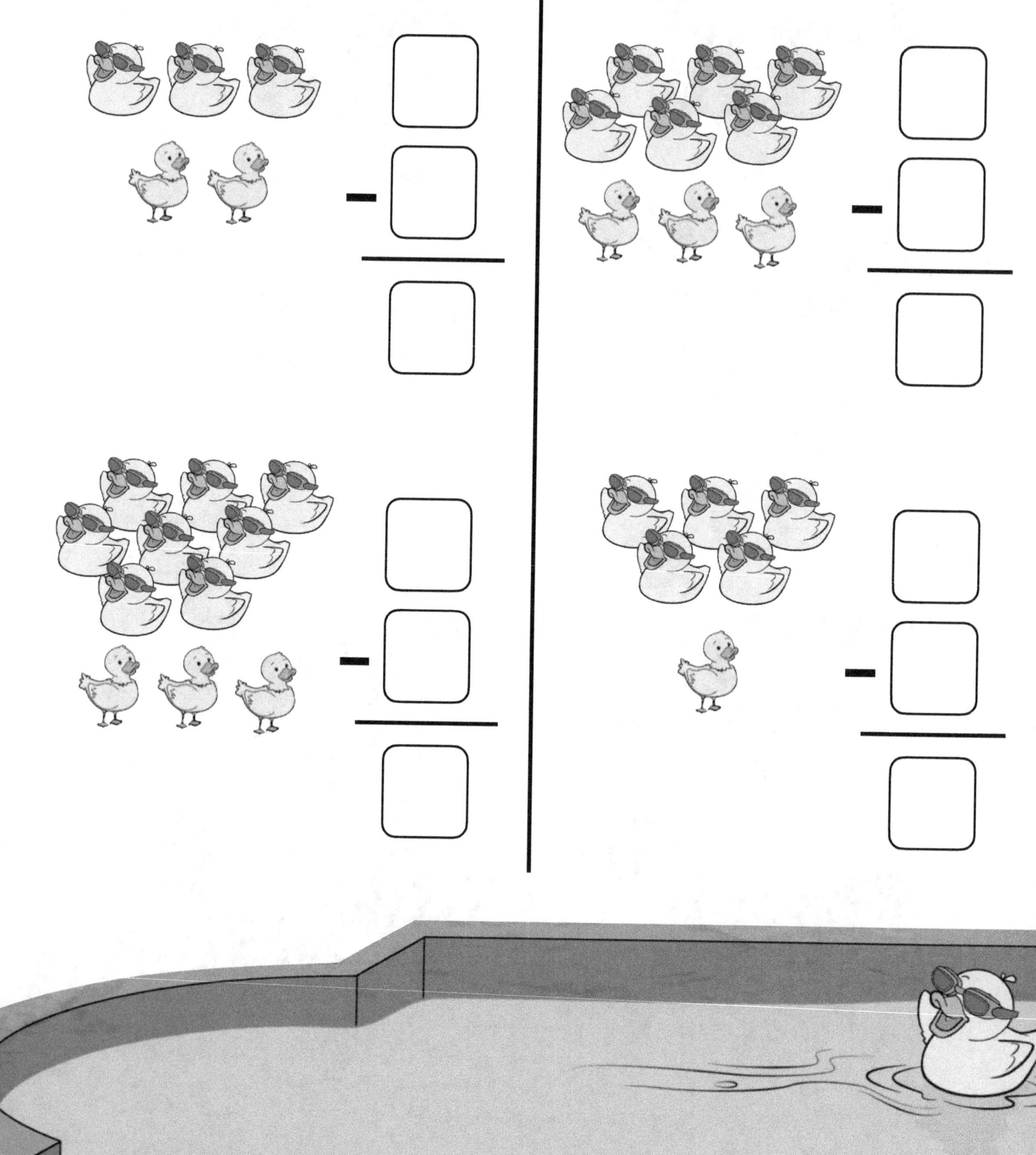

Farm Animals

Down

Across

Farm Finish

Help Beckham with the alphabet by filling in the missing letters on the farm animals.

Which Has Fewer?

Circle the group that has fewer.

Can you form a sentence?

Use these words to form a sentence. Write it on the lines below.

the

pig

bath

needs

stinky

a

_____

- -

_____

- -

_____

The Four Seasons

Draw a line to match the right picture to the correct season.

 · · Winter

 · · Spring

 · · Summer

 · · Autumn

Fun with Math

Write the correct answer inside the balloon.

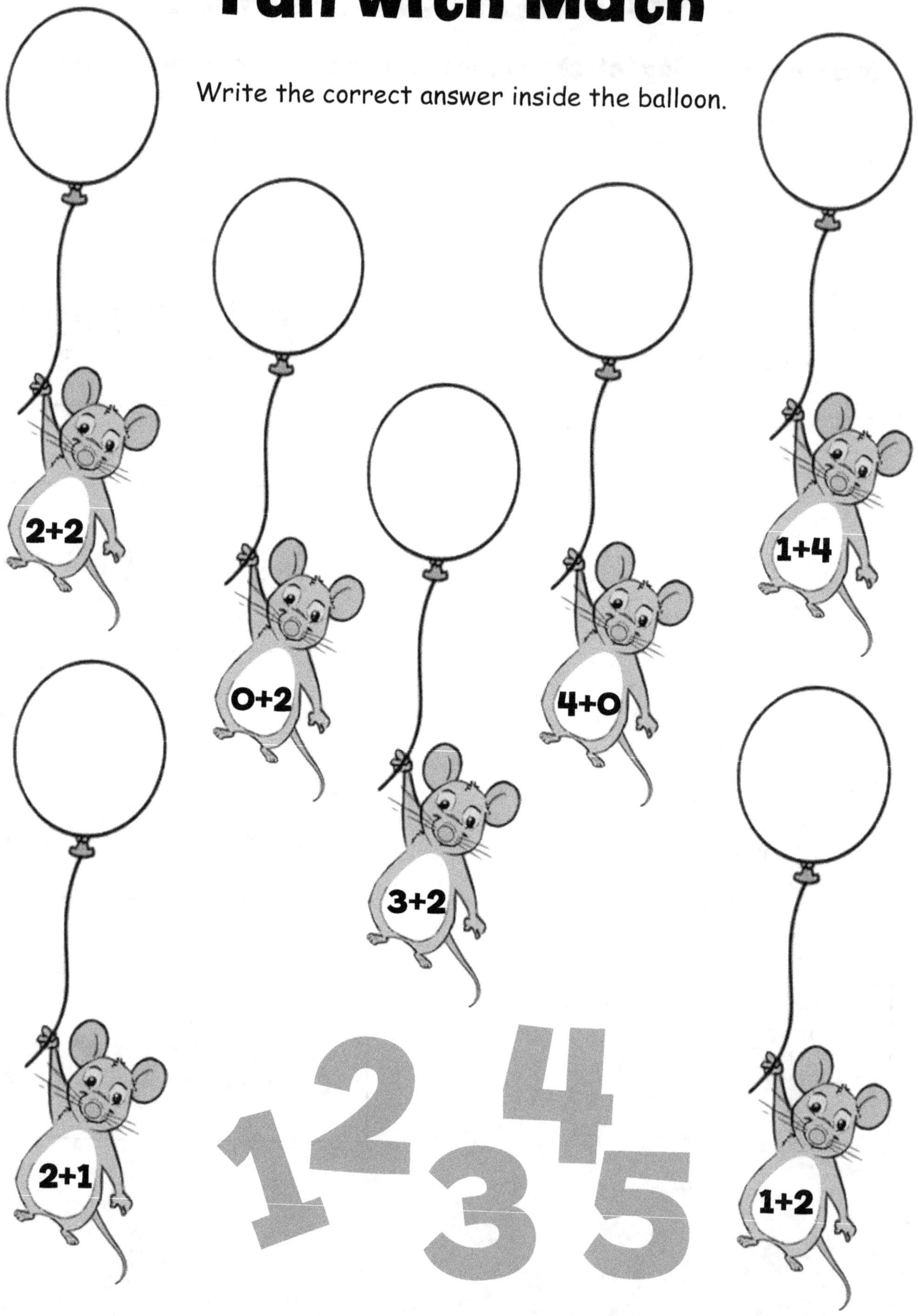

2+2

0+2

4+0

1+4

2+1

3+2

1 2 4 3 5

1+2

Groups of Eight

Draw a line from the number 8 to each group of 8.

Look, Practice, Spell

Look at the picture. **Practice** the beginning letter. **Spell** the word for each picture.

Pp   pig

Cc   chicken

Dd   dog

Rr   rabbit

Cc   cow

Bb   balloon

Rr   rat

Pp   pony

Gg   goose

Ll   lamb

Main Idea

Look at each picture. Read each sentence.
Circle the sentence that best describes what is happening in the picture.

The pig is thinking.	
The pig is stinky.	
Beckham is happy.	

The pig is playing in the mud with Beckham.	
The pig and Beckham are happy.	
The pig wants to swim.	

The goose is riding on a skateboard.	
The goose is wearing roller skates.	
The goose is going to a baseball game.	

The chicken loves to fly.	
The chicken is being dropped by a drone.	
The chicken is eating corn.	

Make Your Own Compound Words

sun   bow   skate   man   house

dog   board   glasses   rain   mail

1. _____

2. _____

3. _____

4. _____

5. _____

Modes of Transportation

There are a number of ways that you can move one place to another. Using the word bank below, write down how each of the animals arrives to Beckham Grey's event.

roller skates   skateboard   balloon
scooter   drone   bike

1. Goose rides a _____.

2. Pony wears _____.

3. Rat hangs from a _____.

4. Moo wobbles in on a _____.

5. Chicken drops from a _____.

6. A lamb rolls in on a _____.

Months of the Year

Color all of the
SUMMER months

Color all of the
FALL months

Color all of the
WINTER months

Color all of the
SPRING months

January

February

March

April

May

June

July

August

September

October

November

December

Measure It!

The skateboard is about _____ inch(es) long.

The goggles are about _____ inch(es) long.

The hat is about _____ inch(es) long.

The tub is about _____ inch(es) long.

The cow is about _____ inch(es) long.

Fill in the MISSING numbers on the sheep.

Moo's Way Home

Moo, the cow, needs help finding her way back to the barn.
Color the **squares** and **circles** along the path that get her home.

More or Less?

Compare the two numbers in each row. Trace the correct word
"more" or "less" to complete the sentence correctly.

6 is | more / less | than 3

3 is | more / less | than 5

7 is | more / less | than 2

2 is | more / less | than 1

8 is | more / less | than 9

Color every number eight.
How many did you find?

Your Answer

One Less

Write the number in the box that is ONE less.

☐	9
☐	5
☐	7
☐	3
☐	6
☐	2
☐	4

One More

Write the number in the box that is ONE more.

8 ☐

2 ☐

6 ☐

4 ☐

1 ☐

5 ☐

3 ☐

+1

+1

+1

Out of Sight Words

the Read it.

Say the word out loud.

THE Color it.

Color the word.

Trace it.

the

Trace the word.

Clap it.

(1) (2) (3)

How many syllables are in the word?
Color in the correct number.

Write it.

Write the word.

Spell it.

Spell the word.

Find it.
Find the word and color it.

tie	thee	tke
ten	the	tell

Say it, again!

the
t-h-e

Say the word, again.
Then spell it out loud.

Poetry Challenge

Read the passage from the book *The Adventures of Beckham Grey: The Farm Challenge* and circle each S that you see.

Overhead, a balloon floated down, joining the scene.
A gray farm rat was tightly gripping the string.

Rat gently landed at Beckham's feet.
"Well, hello!" Blurted Beckham. "You have friends to meet."

The farm animals began gathering around.
Thank goodness the cat was far out of town.

Sadly, she had a bad tooth with a crack,
but at least the rat couldn't be her afternoon snack.

me-OWWWW!

I found _____ S's.

Problem Solving

Directions: Read each story problem and solve.

There are 2 cows in the field and 2 more in the barn.

How many cows are on the farm?

_____ cows

The pony has 4 skates. He loses 1.

How many skates are left?

_____ skates

The rat had 6 balloons. 4 of them popped.

How many balloons does rat have now?

_____ balloons

1 pig is in the tub and 2 pigs are in the yard.

How many pigs in all?

_____ pigs

Proper Punctuation

BECKHAM needs help putting the end punctuation mark for each sentence. Help him complete each sentence by adding a period (.), exclamation point (!), or question mark (?).

1. Pig really stinks

2. Does Pig need a bubble bath

3. Who did not join the farm challenge

4. What color were Pony's skates

5. It is going to be a fun day

6. Rat floated down on a balloon

7. The farm animals began gathering around

8. A tug-of-war will be fun

9. They pulled and pulled to win the game

10. What a lovely adventure they had that day

Questions? Questions?

Beckham hid question marks everywhere in the picture below.
Can you find them?
Draw a circle around all eleven.

Rhyme Time

Choose EIGHT colors. Using the colors, create eight
groups of rhyming words by coloring them the same color.

feet	jam	play	lamb
crack	sleep	head	snack
top	said	pink	grey
day	meet	sheep	hop
pop	way	stink	pled

Searching for Words

Letters have gone missing. Can you help Beckham Grey find them?
Fill in the blanks to complete each word. Practice saying the words out loud.

☐ oose

☐ icken

☐ ony

☐ uck

☐ ike

b   p   ch   g   d

Shapes and More Shapes

Learn your shapes by tracing the lines. Can you say the name of each shape?

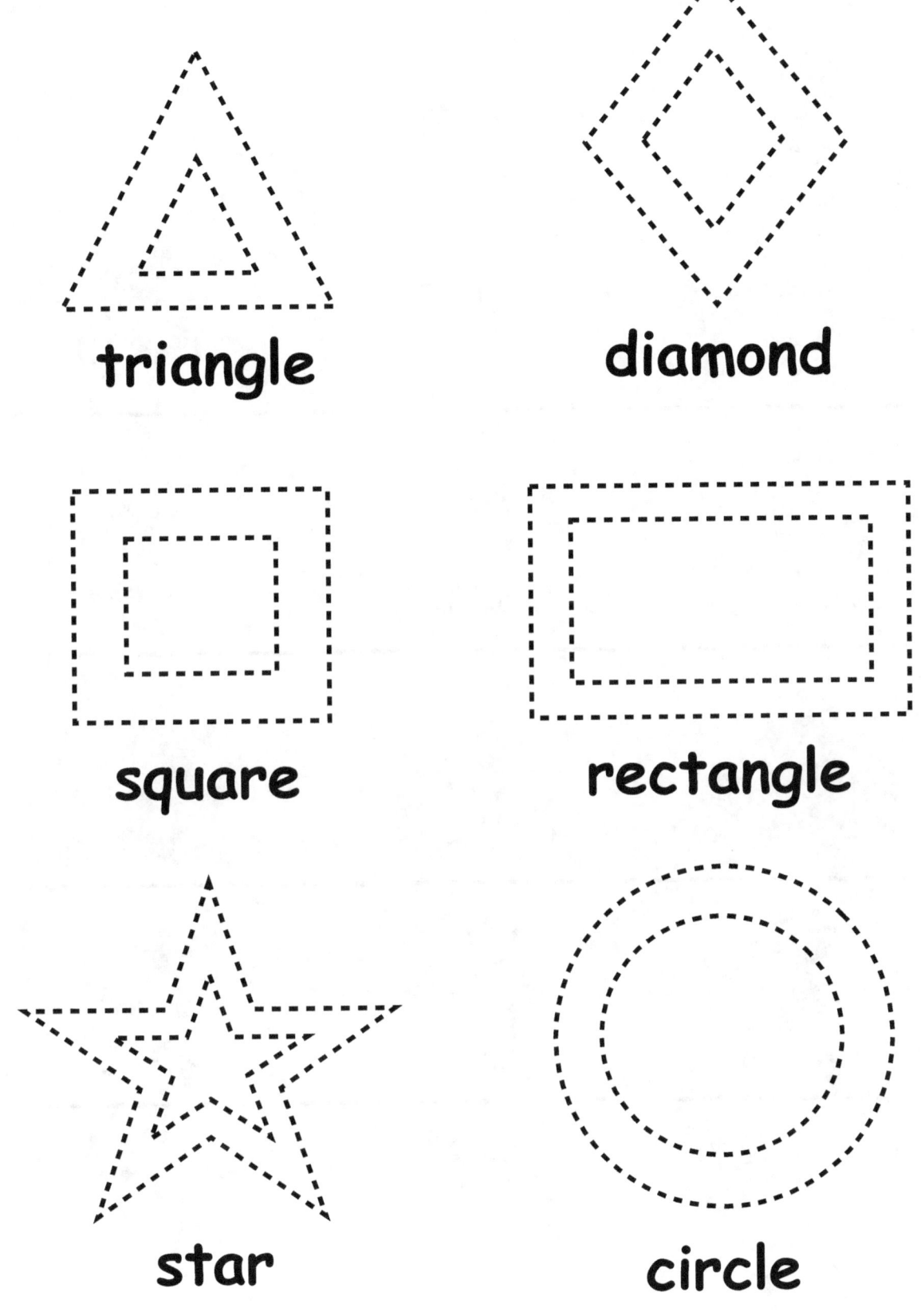

triangle

diamond

square

rectangle

star

circle

Something's Missing

Circle the picture in each row that has something missing.
Can you draw the missing parts?

Spelling Bee

Circle the word that is spelled correctly for each picture.

	chichen chicken chiken
	goose gouse guse
	ponie pony poney
	baith bath baph
	singe sign sing
	balune balloon baloon
	rat ratt rate
	shep shepe sheep

Taking Shape

Count the number of each shape. Color them as you count.
Answer the question.

How many ...

triangles? _____

circles? _____

stars? _____

squares? _____

rectangles? _____

Telling Time

Draw a line to match the clocks that display the same times.

Pig gets a bath at 10:30.

Moo wobbles in on a bike at 11:05.

It's 10:00. Beckham and Gigi go outside to play.

It's time for lunch at noon.

Rat drops in at 11:15 and is ready to play.

Use the picture to help you unscramble the letters.
Write the word in the space provided.

	trbabi	-------------------------------
	gpi	-------------------------------
	ooges	-------------------------------
	nekcich	-------------------------------

What Weighs Less?

Circle the object that is lighter.

What Doesn't Belong?

Circle the things that don't belong in Beckham's backyard. Then color the picture.

Word Match

Help Beckham, Gigi, and Charlie match the words to their definitions. Draw a line from each word to its meaning.

Cling	Cried out; screamed.
Hooted	A sound of interest or concern; a clicking sound made with the tongue.
Tangled	Smiled happily.
Lively	To grasp; to stick to.
Cluck	Location; picture; setting; situation.
Twine	Twisted; trapped.
Beamed	A strong string.
Ultimate	Delightful; charming
Scene	Enjoyable; entertaining.
Adorable	Latest; extreme.

Word UP!

Do you know the word for each definition?
Need help? Refer to the Glossary in the book **The Adventures of Beckham Grey: The Farm Challenge.**

ACROSS

2   Barely heard; distant.
7   Flew; whirled.
9   A title to something.
11 Nervously excited.
14 Surprised; puzzled.
15 Animals; critters.
17 Dropped down; fell.
19 To grasp; to stick to.

DOWN

1   A strong string.
3   Called out; exclaimed.
4   Uncommon; different.
5   Competition; match.
6   Twisted; trapped.
8   Engaging; compelling
10 Holding firmly.
12 Shaking; teetering.
13 Grunt; laugh.
16 Confirmed; positively stated.
18 Gentle; calm; delicate.
19 Group; crowd.

Write a Question

Complete each sentence by filling in the first word using the word bank at the bottom. End each sentence with a question mark.

1. _____ you read *The Farm Challenge* ___

2. _____ delivered the stinky pig ___

3. _____ was Pig in the bath ___

4. _____ was the bubble bath ___

5. _____ Pig have a curly tail ___

6. _____ animal arrived next ___

The Adventures of YOU and Beckham Grey

Join Beckham on an adventure. Draw a picture of yourself with Beckham. Then add some farm animals of your own. Color the picture.

Now go create your own adventure!

Stinky Pig

Follow the path to get Stinky Pig to the washtub. You can pick up only two of his friends along the way. Don't get lost! Color Beckham and Pig when Pig's all clean.

START

END

First, Second, Third

Have you read the book *The Adventures of Beckham Grey: The Farm Challenge*? Cut out each picture below and paste them in order of when each animal arrived to the challenge (first, second, and third).

first

Second

Third

Farm Animal Match

Cut out each of the tiles. Turn them upside down and mix them up.
Take turns turning two tiles over at a time. If you find a match,
you keep it. If you don't, turn the tiles back over. Take turns until
all tiles are matched.

		chicken	rabbit
		goose	sheep
		cow	pony
		rat	pig
		duck	dog